Patterns

of

Australia

Bronwyn Bancroft

LITTLE HARE

As an artist, when I look at the world around me, I often see the micro patterns and details which make up the larger picture. This is particularly the case when I look at different natural environments. Some people can walk through the bush or the desert, or swim in the river or the ocean, and see nothing, while others see life all around them. It has to do with perception and observation. Traditional Aboriginal art can be understood in this way too, as it also has two layers. The outer story is the surface, the public "story" of the artwork; but what most people can't see is the inner story, that which is hidden, secret, sacred. Only the initiated, or people from that clan, know how to read the inner story.

The pictures in this book also work as layers. They are an introduction to how I see some of the diverse and beautiful landscapes that make up Australia. Remember to look beneath the patterns, the outer story, and you will see so much more than is visible at first sight. Although I am not creating traditional Aboriginal art, my work is influenced by the stories and artwork of my ancestors. I see myself as creating another platform from which to read Aboriginal Australia, creating a new way of seeing— my way of seeing—while drawing on the old ways.

The first picture, on the page opposite, is a good example. It's a picture of a homecoming, with patterns and symbols that are very important to me. At the bottom of the picture are diamonds, representing New South Wales. This particular symbolic design works across the different language groups. The clearing within the diamonds represents home for the eagle. Above the land I have painted the Clarence River, which is where I come from, and along the river I have put circles to represent communities. When wedge-tailed eagles come to you, it means "welcome to country". I have depicted one here to welcome you to my book.

PATTERNS OF THE SKY

Lots of people see "pictures" in clouds, and I wanted to convey that sense of transformation.
The clouds here are a dense design element, moving together, shifting, changing.

As well as what you would expect to see in flight—the cockatoo, a galah, a kite, a king parrot, a dragonfly, a butterfly and bees—there is also a boomerang, representing the old times, along with contemporary airborne figures, like the parachutist and the hot-air balloons.

PATTERNS OF THE BUSH
To me, the inanimate is as important as the animate in the bush,
and that is why the rocks I've painted appear as organic as the tree trunks.
The pattern of circles represents chlorophyll, and how nature constantly recreates itself.

Animals disappear in the bush, becoming part of their surroundings. Maybe you can see an echidna, a frill-necked lizard, a rock wallaby, a magpie, a sugar glider, a red goshawk, a wedge-tailed eagle, a blue-tongue lizard, a blue wren and skinks.

PATTERNS OF THE NIGHT
Lying out in the bush at night, looking up at the sky with stars as your only illumination, you have to listen for the animals you can't see.

What can you hear, rustling among the leaves? Perhaps a koala, a possum, an owl, a bat, a toad, a carpet snake and a spider.

PATTERNS OF THE DESERT

When I think of the desert, I think of movement. The very air seems to move
with flickering heat and sand particles blown by the wind.

The animals that live in this harsh environment move through the country in search of food.
There is a surprising amount of life in the desert—you might see a red kangaroo, a scorpion,
an emu, a wombat, a bilby, a snake, a goanna, a brumby and wedge-tailed eagles.

PATTERNS OF WILDFLOWERS

I have put the wildflowers in a desert setting, to show that even though a landscape may appear barren, it doesn't mean there's nothing there. For in the ever-changing seasonal landscape, a barren land may burst into bloom. Suddenly, there is abundance.

The wildflowers I have painted are not particular to any specific place;
they come from all over Australia. Some you will be familiar with, like the
Sturt's desert pea, a waratah, wattle, kangaroo paws. But can you recognise callistemons,
sundew, phebalium, fringe myrtle, emu bush and snow daisies?

PATTERNS OF THE RIVER

The old stories tell of the rainbow serpent that went through the land and created the rivers,
and you can see the sinuous shape of the serpent behind the patterns of this picture.
The pattern of bubbles represents effervescence, and the freshness of the water.

Hidden behind the surface bubbles are a crocodile, a water snake, a turtle,
a water spider, fish, a yabby, a platypus, a crane, ducks and tadpoles.

PATTERNS OF THE WETLANDS
This picture reminds me of the time I spent in the gorges around the Kimberley Ranges.
The repeating pattern of the sun's rays symbolises the sunrise in early morning,
and hundreds of birds and animals starting the day.

In this habitat that is both land and water, you might see a water monitor, a rock wallaby, a heron, a crayfish, a sea eagle, a magpie goose, fish, brolgas and black swans.

PATTERNS OF THE RAINFOREST

I grew up with the rainforest of the Bundjalung State Forest as my home,
so I can paint it very fluently. The rainforest is like nature's cave—its damp,
dark canopy feels almost nocturnal, and the colours are muted.

In the foliage, bush rats, a kingfisher, a witchetty grub, a butterfly, a frog,
a snake, a goanna and a cassowary are hiding.

PATTERNS OF THE OCEAN

The tumbling curves of this picture convey a sense of being within the waves,
as well as representing the cyclical nature of life in the ocean. If we treat the ocean
with respect, we will be able to see the same picture in 20 000 years.

The ocean is mysterious, dark; we never know what's underneath the waves.
There could be a turtle, a starfish, a stingray, a squid, a seahorse, a sea snake, a shark.
Looking through the waves to the sky there are ocean birds, like seagulls.

PATTERNS OF THE REEF

When you look at a stretch of water, you can see beautiful shimmering colours playing across the surface. I have represented these as ribbons, like strands of soft coral.

Beneath the surface are dolphins, a starfish, a clam, a diver,
a shark, a whale, shells and tropical fish.

First published in 2005
First published in paperback 2006

National Library of Australia
Cataloguing-in-Publication entry

Bancroft, Bronwyn.
Patterns of Australia.

For children.
ISBN 978 1 921049 70 5.

ISBN 1 921049 70 7.

1. Landscape - Australia - Juvenile literature.
2. Landscape - Australia - Pictorial works. 3. Australia -
Juvenile literature. 4. Australia - Pictorial works.
I. Title.

994

Designed by Serious Business
Produced by Phoenix Offset, Hong Kong
Printed in China

5 4 3 2 1